Best Selling Author

Conversations of The Heart

An Interactive Prayer Book

Jasmine D. Felder, M.Ed

Conversations of the Heart

An Interactive Prayer Book

Jasmine D. Felder

Motivated Minds Publishing

www.motivatedmindspublishing.com

Copyright © 2021 by Jasmine D. Felder

Published by Motivated Minds Publishing, Macon Georgia

www.motivatedmindspublishing.com

All rights reserved. No part of this book may be reproduced, stored in a retrieval system, or transmitted in any form or by any means electronic, mechanical photocopying, recording, scanning, or otherwise except as permitted under Section 107 or 108 of the 1976 United States Copyright Act, without either prior written permission from the author.

Limit of Liability / Disclaimer. The advice and strategies contained herein may not be suitable for your situation. You should consult with a professional where appropriate. Neither the Publisher and or the author shall be liable for any loss of profit or any other commercial damages, including but not limited to special, incidental, consequential, or other damages.

Scripture and Bible references taken from the New King James Version®. Copyright © 1982 by Thomas Nelson. Used by permission. All rights reserved.

Motivated Minds Publishing and products are available through Amazon, other bookstores, and Motivated Minds Publishing. To contact Motivated Minds Publishing, visit www.motivatedmindspublishing.com.

ISBN -978-0-578-90536-5

Printed in the United States of America.

Table of Contents

Dedication 1
Introduction 3
Prayer 6

Day One: Fear 8
Prayer: Fear Removed Prayer 9
Activity: Let's Talk Fear, ... 10

Day Two: Relationships 11
Prayer: The Right Relationships Prayer 13
Activity: Let's Talk Relationships, ... 14

Day Three: Discomfort 16
Prayer: From Uncomfortable to Trusting Prayer 17
Activity: Discomfort Activity 18

Day Four: Why Me 19
Prayer: Old Me Versus New Me Prayer 20
Activity: Transformation of Me Activity 22

Day Five: Pride 24
Prayer: Healing the Pride Prayer 25
Activity: Pride Versus Healing Diary Activity 26

Day Six: Loss..27
Prayer: Battle of Emotions Prayer 29
Activity: Power of Release Activity 30

Day Seven: Cycles of Hurt 32
Prayer: Going in Circles Prayer 34
Activity: The Never-Ending Circle Activity 35

Day Eight: Fixer 36
Prayer: Fix it Jesus, Not Me Prayer 38
Activity: Fixing the Interior of the Heart.....................39

Day Nine: The Strength of Your Tree 41
Prayer: Roots Versus Branches Prayer 43
Activity: Roots Versus Branches Activity....................45

Day Ten: Conversations of the Heart 47
Prayer: Final Prayer 49
Activity: Conversations of the Heart Final Activity.....50

Letter to My Readers..51
About the Author..53

Dedication

I dedicate my life to God. He has shown me that he will provide for me if I faint not. I love you Lord, and I pray you continue to use me as a vessel.

Shakina Lashawn Armstrong Smith, my sister and now my angel, it has been six years since you left this Earth. You did not get to see me accomplish my greatest achievements because you were taken so soon. I miss your sisterly advice. I could use your feisty attitude sometimes and I know you are probably saying, "come on Jasmine, toughen up." Keep watching over us please. I will keep working and being the woman you always encouraged me to be. I love you!

Anna Mae Felder. Queen, the fact is I miss you. It has been a long time since I had you 100 percent but, having a small piece of you is better than not having you at all. Grandma, from day one of my life, you have been there. You were the only consistent family my mom and I had, especially in the physical sense. I miss your feisty attitude as well. I miss mom, you, and I sitting in the living room watching movies. I miss going to garage sales with you and then going to the Waffle House after. I miss the proud smile you wore when I achieved an accomplishment. Lady, I miss you and I am so hurt by your absence that sometimes I do not think this part of my heart will heal. Thank you for all of your knowledge and wisdom. Until we meet again.

Glenda Delores McGriff! My mother, my best friend, my confidant, my counselor, my challenger. You may not know it but I admire your strength and I constantly try to duplicate it. Thank you for being an amazing mother and GiGi. You have accepted me as I am over and over. You open yourself up to me without a second thought and I so appreciate you. The passion you show, the love you give, and the concern you provide tells me I will always have a supporter. You are willing to always go the extra mile and anyone who messes with your baby is on your list lol. I hope I can continue to make you proud, and I pray I can be half the mother you are.

A'Lani!!! My Lani Poo. My Londyn Bridges. My sweet, sweet baby girl. You are the motivation behind me. Before you, my life really did not have meaning. I look at all I have accomplished in the short year of you being born and I am amazed but, it is only because of you. You are a replica of my attitude and personality. You say what you mean and mean what you say (even if no one understands) lol. Your dance moves, smile, photogenic profile, sweetness, and kindness is a blessing. You are what I prayed for and I pray God continues to allow me to be the best mother ever!

In Memory to a man of many titles that are not limited in one aspect but matter so much. Husband, son, brother, friend, god-father, biker, and more. Rest in Heaven, Michael (Mad Max) Hamilton. To my best friend, his amazing wife, Luciyonna Hamilton, thank you for showing me the true epitome of a strong woman. I will always love you and value our friendship.

Introduction

Prayer is often seen as a routine, a responsibility, a requirement, or a means to receive. When we pray many times, it comes from a selfish standpoint. We are asking God, "why?" "what can you do for me?" or "how?" We behave in a manner that tells God "you owe me." Now of course, we should go to God with our desires, our needs, and tell him our inner-most secrets. However, is the relationship one-sided? Do we only go to God when our lives have taken a drastic negative change? Do we say, "Thank you for this day God?" before jumping into our list of demands? I believe the problem most of us face is our relationship with God has shifted and He is not the one who has moved. You have to think of it in the aspect of a romantic relationship or even a friendship. If the relationship is one-sided, will it ever prevail? If only one person is supportive, loving, dedicated, accountable, and loyal will the relationship be successful? The answer is no! No one can continue to give, give, give, and allow someone else to take, take, take and there not be high levels of toxicity. The same is with God; He loves us dearly but, our purpose is to serve him but, we act as if his purpose is to serve us. I am inclined to say, check your relationship with God on an individual basis and you will be able to see why you are incurring some valley's. Now that is not to say if your relationship with God is strong, you will not incur dark days because you will but, when you realize truly where your help comes from, when you realize why prayer and communing with God is important, and when you realize that GOD is your focus, he is your strength, and He is your help those darks days become light because you know who is at the end of the tunnel.

This prayer book is designed as a personal journey we are taking together with God. I am sure we all can agree the year 2020 came with many hills and valleys. There were so many low points that we all have asked in some way, shape or form "WHY"? The year 2020 was supposed to be the year of blessings, great manifestation, profit, productivity, and increase. The question is was it not? 2020 and 2021 came with a lot of loss, plagues, sickness, monetary declines, brokenness in families and relationships, and fear. However, did it also not come with unexpected blessings, monetary gain, additions to families, favor on jobs, promotions, increased family time, and tables turning for understanding? I believe God uses unexpected disaster to show us in modern-day times that He can and still will turn dry bones into great manifestation. I lost sight of many things in this past year and a half and this prayer book is my personal prayer to God. Moreover, I am speaking for my family, friends, colleagues, and strangers from near and by. The troubles we face are not always given with the intent to harm but the encouragement to overcome. This is a prayer book of intent. I invite you to read each prayer on its specified day, follow the interactive pages that follow, and hold yourself accountable to the changes God is ready to make in your life. The first step to making any relationship successful is communication and that is exactly what we are going to do on this journey, communicate with God. All of our relationships with

God are different and we commune differently. Trust yourself and do not be afraid of the greatness that is about to transpire; you deserve it!

Prayer

Father God,

I pray that You work through me to fulfill Your will. Allow me to say the right statements at the right time. For the person reading this who is misguided, allow these prayers to guide them Lord. For the person who feels alone, allow this book to help them feel your presence. For the broken-hearted, Jesus, give them peace that transcends all understanding. Let me be a vessel, Jesus. Allows my trials to speak to them, to let them know they are not alone. Let my brothers and sisters in Christ feel the tears and pains together so we can experience the joys together! When two or three are called in Your name, You are in the midst. So Heavenly father, join us!

Lord, as You hold us accountable, let us hold You accountable. We know You love it when we can recite Your word back to You. So, Father, we are not leaving until You bless us! You said You would never leave us nor forsake us. You said You would give us beauty for our ashes. So, Father, in the late midnight hour when those closest to us are sleep, remind us You do not sleep or slumber. Calm us. Go before us and make it all better. Wrap us in your arms and wipe the tears that may fall from our eyes. The great thing is I know You can, and I know You will. You do not lie, so if You said it, we can believe it.

I pray that this book does Your intended purpose and work. Reach long and far. Touch those that do not even know they have fallen from your arms. Let this prayer book arrive as an unexpected blessing where it needs to be. Remove my wants and remove my desires to do Your will.

In Jesus Name,

Amen.

Day One

Fear

Fear is often the culprit that keeps us from executing on God's will. We wonder, "Can I do it?" "How will I do it?" and "Why me?" These questions keep us in bondage for so long that we begin to question our worth, we limit ourselves, and we become potential bound instead of living in our destiny. Fear is our worst enemy because it seeps into our minds and makes us believe and imagine circumstances that are not there. We have to remember the devil was once an angel, so he knows the Bible just as well or better than many of us. Many of us have what I call falsified fear. We have allowed life and people to make us afraid of tackling our goals. We see a challenge and instead of believing we can conquer it, we listen to the naysayers and run away?

Think have you ever had a goal but listened to someone doubt you, or even talked yourself out of it? Did you ever want to achieve something but thought that it was too high of a goal to reach? Are you scared to be the first in your family, among your friends, in your school, or first-ever? Fear can paralyze us due to its capacity to limit our thinking. My prayer today is that we rise over fear. We stop believing in fear. We challenge fear. We conquer fear.

Fear Removed Prayer

Father God,

I pray that the person reading this is no longer imprisoned by fear. I pray that fear is released from their mind, body, and soul. I pray for strength among their minds. I pray that they realize their past does not define them. I pray that their past self does not cause them to be apprehensive of the successful, prosperous, and confident future self they are destined to be. I pray the anxiety and concern is replaced with confidence and strength. I pray that their best self is revealed and no longer fights what is meant for them. I pray they realize their worth and I pray generations of lies, unfortunate events, and fear is broken.

In Jesus Name,
Amen.

Let's Talk Fear,

Name 5 Things You Are Afraid Of?

1. _____

2. _____

3. _____

4. _____

5. _____

What Are Your 3 Short Term Goals (Meet Within Two Years)

1. _____

2. _____

3. _____

What Are Your 2 Long Term Goals (Meet Within Five Years)

1. _____

2. _____

Personal Statement Against Fear

_____

Day Two

Relationships

Let's be honest; relationships sometimes cause the heaviest burden we will experience in life. God intended for us to have relationships; the sad truth is just not with everyone. We open up ourselves to the wrong people and problems arise solely due to the company we keep. Our relationships range from family to spouses, to significant others, to friends and colleagues. Relationships are hard typically because someone does more or puts in more work than the other. Someone always feels undervalued in comparison to the other. We must include God in all of our relationships, whether they are personal or professional. Relationships take the wrong turn when God is not included. We feel alone, taken advantage of, lied to, and manipulated because we do not pray over the people we allow into our lives.

Now think about your relationships that drain you. Think about the relationships where you feel as if you are doing all of the work. Are these individuals waiting until you do everything or is it a partnership? Do you feel as if you are being poured into? Relationships are 50 /50 but, to ensure the success of the relationship, both parties must give 100 percent. Consider your closest family and friends; are they individuals who add to your life? Do you feel encouraged when you are around them? Are you at peace in their presence?

On the contrary, do you feel drained when you are around them? Are the important relationships in your life taking your smile, your happiness, and your peace? Trust that God never wants to see us hurt. Flags always appear. Discernment is always placed in our spirits. Are you listening?

The Right Relationships Prayer

Lord,

I pray that You touch the individuals reading this message. I know You designed relationships for us to enjoy. You want us to have friends and be in love; however, none of these relationships should mean more to us than You or be stronger than the relationship we have with You. I ask Father that You put the right people in our lives. You know the hearts of everyone we come into contact with. Strengthen our spirit of discernment so that our spirit matches Yours. Order our steps to where we can hear from you clearly. Please remove the people from our lives who serve us no good and give us the strength to accept the termination of these relationships.

In Psalm 35, you listened to David mourn relationships Lord. You heard his cry from hurt and betrayal. We ask now Lord that You hear our cry. Protect us from those who prey on our quiet demeanors, warm-hearted personalities, and kindness. Moreover, please continue to build relationships with those we need in our lives. Help us to be just as great to them as we want them to be to us. Make sure we are reciprocating the love, support, patience, and dedication we want in return. Help us to listen more than we speak.

In Jesus Name,
Amen.

Let's Talk Relationships,

Think about the closest people in your lives; put their names in this box.

For your own use, allot one point for every time this year that particular individual supported you, made you feel their love, or they added to your life in a positive way.

Now deduct one point for every time that same person made you feel less than, took you for granted, and impacted your life in a negative way.

Does the good outweigh the bad?

Conversations of The Heart

Day Three

Discomfort

Discomfort is an uncomfortable feeling. We hope to never feel it, we push it away, and we run away from it. While the feeling of discomfort is something we hope to avoid forever, its presence provides a necessity. In my previous book Finding Your Vision in the Darkness, I discuss how God many times uses us in our dark place. As humans, it is common for us to perceive we have to have our lives all together or at least present it this way. Social media shows us an alternative reality of life. We see the glitz and glam of life, but we do not see the scrutiny, heartbreak, loss, and more it took to get there. In today's modern time, we want success without hard work.

Whether we want to see it as fortunate or not, God allows situations to cause us discomfort at times to make us better. This discomfort can be a part of His master plan for our better or even the result and consequence of our own actions. Discomfort can many times be a blessing in disguise. Think about Job in the Bible; He lost EVERYTHING and was even told to curse God. However, he remained faithful and loyal to God and he received double for his trouble. If you feel like you are in an uncomfortable place, talk to God. Tell Him how you feel. Ask Him to show you the way. Always trust that His plans are to prosper us and not harm us.

From Uncomfortable to Trusting Prayer

Jesus,

Life is so different in today's world. The expectations have changed and heightened to an outrageous degree. Many people are comparing their lives to each other or living a falsified lifestyle. We have a distorted view of reality: when hard times come, we believe we are the only people going through; or that hard times relate to punishment versus preparation for success. I ask that you help us to trust you, Lord. Help us to know and believe that you know all and what is best for us. All of your children have different roads to take and while some may seem easier for a while, help us know that individually you are giving us specifically what we need. Although we live in this world, please guide us Lord and remind us that we are not of this world. Yes, we can still laugh, love, have fun, and enjoy but, assist us in remaining vigilant. As You take us from level to level, strengthen us, give us comfort, and end the generational cycles telling us to give up. We pray Father that You nurture our spirit and allow us to see and grow in You. We thank You for the uncomfortable times seeing that we know in a season of uncomforting, we are growing into our best self.

In Jesus Name,

Amen

Discomfort Activity

Thinking about discomfort, what makes you uncomfortable? Think of a few topics or situations that make you uncomfortable. Name them. How would you like to grow out of them?

Topics of Discomfort –

Plans to Grow out of the Discomfort –

Day Four

Questions – Why Me?

Why did I not get the job? Why do my parents not love me? Why can I not find love? Why am I always overlooked? Why me? 2020 was a year of questions. Everyone had a story. Every time you looked around; someone you knew lost a family member. Someone you knew lost their job. Someone you knew had friendship and relationship issues. I believe in the first quarter of 2021; we were already ready to throw in the towel.

So, the question was asked, why me? However, I believe the answer we received was, why not you? It seems insensitive to say when you are going through a horrible situation but, what makes you individually exempt from sorrow like everyone else? However, in an unforeseen situation, something special happens. Families are being restored; faith is being restored, churches started to realize the true power of God was not dependent on the building but dependent on the faith in the people, businesses were created, and more. So, the question of why me begins to come to life and starts to reverse the question and ask, why not you? Why not you be chosen to go through the divorce? Why not you be chosen to be demoted? Why not you be chosen to be betrayed? Do we not realize that Jesus was betrayed by those who sat directly next to him, those whom he healed, those whom he put together again? So again, why not you be used for greater?

Old Me Versus New Me Prayer

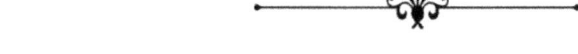

God,

You did something special when you created me, which means I must trust your plans from start to finish. This past year and a half were one of the hardest years I have ever experienced, but You showed me my strength Father. The woman You have called me to be is emerging and I am so proud of my growth. There has been a great deal of shedding and I can see the old me fading away. It frightens me because I have known her for so long and the new me is a stranger. The old me tells me she can change if I give her a little more time while the new me is ready and waiting to fulfill her destiny. The old me tells me she can change the people around her with a little more time and love. The new me says time is up and I have to put myself first.

Lord, as I transform, help me to let go of the old things, old favorites, and old mindsets. Help me to not be so hard on myself during this transition, seeing that old habits die hard. However, help me to know this change is necessary. As I see the ashes blow away, help to transform beautifully and love the change gracefully. I know You have great things in store for me. I know You are sitting in Heaven on the throne proud of me. Allow me to have moments of flashbacks for growth purposes only, to confirm how far I have come. However, do not ever let me look back, Lord in sadness or regret of the choices made for my benefit and good. Thank You, Lord,

In Jesus Name,

Amen

Transformation of Me Activity

Think about your current mindset and where you want to go. This activity will have a slot allotted for what you would say versus how you want to start thinking.

Ready

Set

GO!

What I Currently Say?	What I Want to Say?
Example: I hate where I am in life.	Example: I am not satisfied with my current standing but, I know with hard work I will get there.

Day Five

Pride

The Bible says that pride comes before destruction. In my personal opinion, pride has two sides. The first side is the typical framework of pride that we all know of, which consists of stubbornness and relentless characteristics. However, there is a type of pride that is not purposefully prideful. This type of pride comes from the hurt, the pain, and the disappointment that life throws our way.

In life, we lose sometimes, we are picked over, and sometimes others are chosen in areas we feel we should be chosen in. Rejection is an emotion most people do not take well and when we feel rejected, we hold on to it. This type of pride tends to simmer when hurtful situations have not healed. As a result, no one can give a person in this situation any advice and a complex mentality is formed. Hurt people, hurt others, but no matter what happens, there is no excuse that can be formed that justifies any behavior that hurts anyone. Having pride will cause anyone to lose relationships, have a falsified sense of reality, and eventually, if not corrected, self-destruct. Realize where you are pridefully and allow God to heal the hurt from it before it corrupts.

Healing the Pride Prayer

Lord,

There are so many feelings and emotions that we go through daily. Guide our emotions Jesus. Help us to understand that we will face trials. Guide our actions and reactions. Lord, in this modern day, we can have falsified views on reality. However, protect our minds against what is not true. Do not let us focus or harbor on the lives we see other individuals living. Help us to believe with all of our heart that the plans You have for us are the best and no other views or reality can top that. While we would love a life that does not have any ups and downs, the fact is, we will go through situations that test our strength and increase our faith in you. I ask that during those times, Lord You hug us a little more, give us pieces of Your strength, and fill our hearts with love. Any dark places you see in our hearts, mind, and soul, please remove them and cast in Your light.

In Jesus Name,
Amen

Pride Versus Healing Diary Activity

We know that pride, if not healed, can cast darkness over our minds and the way we act. In this activity, you will ponder and recognize a time or times that you let pride take over you. Admit the actions you displayed. Now think, how did you overcome, or did you overcome? When you write your final sentence, place a period after the last word. It is done; it is finished!

_____

_____

_____

_____

_____

_____

_____

_____

Day Six

Loss,

One of the most devasting situations we can partake in or emotions we can feel in life is loss. It could be the loss of a family member, friend, or relationship. Not all losses are physical and many of the losses we face are mental, emotional, and spiritual. The wrong loss especially mental, emotional, or spiritual bound can affect us for years to come if not fixed correctly. Adult women in age but little girls in their mentality are loving the wrong men seeing as though they are still suffering from the absence of their fathers. Communication skills are tainted, intimacy is null in void, and true vulnerableness is extinct because somewhere along the lines, we all lost a part of ourselves. Abandonment in the home as a child, neglect in romantic relationships, and lack of recognition in our everyday lives can piece by piece chip away at a person.

Loss is a powerful battle but, it is a battle that can be won. We must face our deepest and darkest issues with truth and honesty. We have to be honest about the pain in order to grow from it. Many of us are untruthful inwardly with ourselves. Disregarding what we tell others, the dishonesty that we share with ourselves causes us to be internally angry, sad, depressed, and confused. We tend to not be able to hear from God due to the clutter of our minds. It's time to release it, him, her, them, and everything that clouds your mind without purpose and the matching efforts you provide.

Battle of Emotions Prayer

Dear God,

Here we are in our purest form. Lord, we are battling some serious emotions here. We have lost people physically to the causes of life and we have lost people through the emotional standpoint of our hearts. Lord, being honest, we have been lost for years; we have just worn a pretty mask. We have shown the world what was needed temporarily through a smile, grand gesture, accomplishments, and more. However, here today, we are tired, and we are turning over every person, situation, and task to you God. Forgive us for taking detours and not always following you. We ask today that You heal the years and decades of generational curses and pain that have hardened us over the years. We trust in Your will and way and we know that although some people and situations are seasonal, they are needed. We ask that You take over and guide our hearts and emotions. Heal the hurt, frustration, pain, and anger that may come from the losses we have experienced. We ask that You help us trust Your way and always remember that Your plans are to prosper us and not harm us.

In Jesus name we pray,

Amen

Power of Release Activity

I believe we can all attest to the truth that some parts of our personality are not a part of us genetically but, they are more so debris that has attached itself to us. Think about parts of you, your life, situations, and people who have impacted you, maybe in ways that you do not like. You can write their names, the dates of occurrences, or symbols to represent them and what happened. This is your "Power of Release," and as you write your final sentence, you are saying goodbye to the hold that has been on you. Placing the final period will set you free!

Day Seven

Cycles of Hurt

The saying "trouble does not last always" is tried and true. The one great part about experiencing hard times is that the tables will turn (they have no other choice). Knowing there will be a turning point is what helps to increase our faith in those troubling moments. The question is when we are in a cycle of hurt, what do we do? Waiting for the moment of change displays great faith; however, how do we conqueror the challenges that present themselves to us? We all face a cycle or cycles of hurt. Toxicity in a relationship, multiple miscarriages, continued rejection on the job, betrayal from people you would at least expect it from can produce repeated cycles of hurt. Hurt often causes us to shut down and causes refusal to open ourselves up to others again to prevent feeling that feeling ever again. While we may want to blame others, repeated cycles of hurt, especially over the same type of situation, should cause a conversation of hard truths. What part of the blame should we carry for this particular problem?

The truth is some NOT ALL of these situations can be prevented; however, considering some of these situations, it can be perceived that we are not considering our actions. Continuous failed relationships might suggest we are picking the same type of person with identical habits. The individuals may look different, but internally they possess the same qualities. This may sound harsh but, the question is are we looking for a forever love when picking our mates? Are we turning the cheek to the red flags that present themselves to us? Finally, are we rationalizing potential with actuality? Cycles of hurt become repetitive in our lives when we remove God from the front seat and we drive. More than half of the people we know are in careers they hate or are not meant to be in, because we move on emotion rather than importing patience and waiting for our moment. If we slow down, listen, be obedient, and faint, not so many cycles of hurt and pain can be avoided, and we can live the best life God has for us.

Going in Circles Prayer

Father God,

We know that you are Alpha and Omega, the beginning and the end. This means you know every hair strand we have and what our life looks like from the moment of birth until the end. Lord, we have been through so much. I can admit a great deal of pain is self-inflicted. We are so busy trying to create our own version of the life we think we should be living that we miss and erase the blessings we could have found. Help us to remember we are nothing without you. Teach us to confide in you about ALL things. Encourage us to listen to your voice above all. So that when you speak, we listen and obey. Right now, Father we are asking that you remove the repeated cycles of hurt. Break the generational curses. Loose the chains that keep us in bondage. We know that we can do all things through you. Help us to live in our legacy as your child. We know every day will not be a sunny day but, we ask that you give us the strength not to continue to harm ourselves by holding on to the past. We speak a new life and a spiritual transformation like no other!

In Jesus Name,

Amen.

The Never-Ending Circle Activity

In this activity, you will think of situations and people in your life who seem to never bring consistent happiness. Although life is not perfect, repeated cycles of hurt are not what God has intended for us. Each circle represents a person or situation. These circles represent the repeated cycles of the up – down – up – down relationships you may have with someone or something. Be as open or private as you desire. The goal is for you to recognize the pattern and change it, fix it, or let it go!

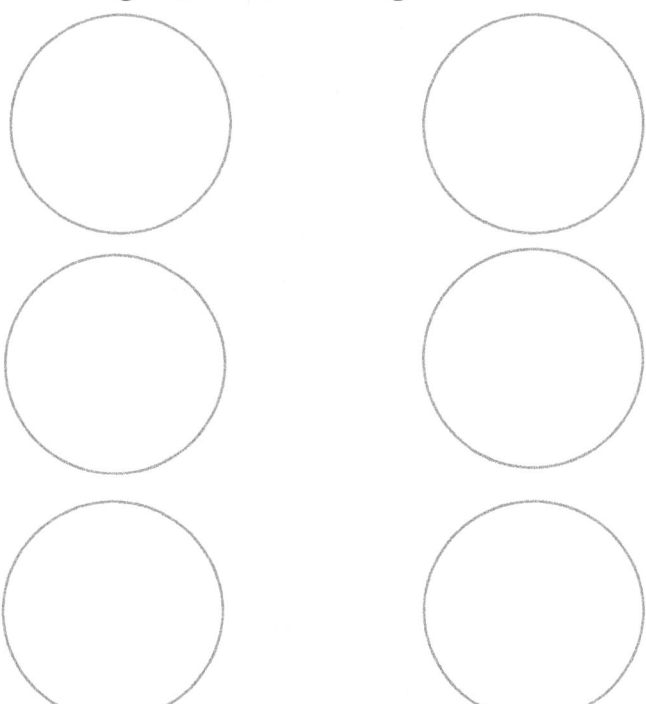

Day Eight

Fixer

In the former show "Scandal," the main character Olivia Pope's job title was a *fixer*. Her job description was to come to the rescue for her employer. No matter what situation they were in, no matter how serious the situation was, and no matter if she believed she could fix the situation or not, she was to find a way to solve the issue completely and be their saving grace. This is an everyday common example of our roles in other individuals' lives. We are their FIXER! We skip, run, and jump for them. Everything they need, we become. We fix their problems as if they are ours. We take on their enemies as if we made them ourselves. We pause our lives as if they would do the same for us. As fixers, we take on the role of being the modern-day Superman and Superwoman. Now to the contrary, it is not always a fact that people "use" fixers. The people we "fix" are not always taking advantage of us purposely. The problem is we have presented ourselves in a manner that speaks to that person "I am available for you," "I am free when it comes to you," "You are more important than anything I have going on," and more.

Outside of actual job positions, we were not created to be a fixer for someone else. It is nothing wrong with helping others, being dependable, or allocating ourselves for others occasionally. The point is to know our limit. How can you be a blessing for someone else before you can be a blessing for yourself? We become tired and drained simply because we are doing more than we should. Sometimes God allows us to feel the hurt, brokenness, and tiredness of being a fixer because he wants us to know that he never intended for that to be our job. Sometimes God does lay on our hearts for us to help others. However, before we make a move, we should consult Him. Moving without consulting God allows others to rely on us more and we prevent God from operating in that person's life how He wants. Our intentions are never the problem; it's questioning our desire to please versus letting God lead.

Fix it Jesus, Not Me Prayer

Lord,

We know we were made in your image. Our want to help and be a blessing to others shows the beauty of our hearts. However, we have extended ourselves too much Lord. We have helped others we were never supposed to help, and we have become a crutch for individuals we were only supposed to help once. Help us to know our worth Lord. Allow us to hear your voice clearly when you give us that nudge. Place in us a discerning spirit so we can identify those who are not supposed to be in our lives. When necessary, bless us to be a blessing to others. Give us the right words and a sincere heart. However, Lord, never let us stay in a situation longer than You intend. Father, we ask that You never allow us to become so consumed that we encourage others to rely on us versus You. We are a vessel for You, but we are not You. You are the fixer, only You can change a person's heart, only You can change a person's behavior, and only You can fix what is broken. We ask that You do.

In Jesus name,

Amen

Fixing the Interior of the Heart

In the previous devotional, we discussed being a fixer, knowing your limits, and not blocking the process God may want a person to go through. In this activity, you will reflect on how you can set limits, set boundaries, and acknowledge your worth in future situations.

How I will Set Limits (family, friends, work, etc.)	How I will Set Boundaries in Relationships

How I will Acknowledge My Worth

Day Nine

The Strength of Your Tree

Being the strong person everyone can count on can take a toll on anyone. The perception is that by being strong you cannot have moments of "weakness." You have to suck up your tears, turn your frown upside down, and laugh to prevent yourself from crying and prove your strength. This type of strength is admirable but, it is also tiring. Always being the *root* for everyone else but, only receiving *branches* from everyone can put a strain on a person. We believe being strong means to give and give and accept others taking and taking. However, this mentality is the exact reason we become burnt out and lose ourselves in the process. Being a good person does not mean we have to accept any form of affection in the hopes of relationships, companionships, or love. The strength of your tree is embedded in your roots. Your roots are the people who love you sincerely, the people who want the best for you, the people who treat you as an equal versus lesser than, and the people who will never allow you to question your position in their lives. When we confuse branches with roots and roots with branches, we open ourselves to unnecessary hurt, despair, and misery.

Everyone is not a permanent figure in our lives. Some people come to teach us; moreover, at times, we are led to educate others.

Temporary relationships can be fun, engaging, and full of temporary enjoyment but, the mistake of eternalness is where we go wrong. Build your tree with more roots than branches and never mistake momentary moments for an infinite existence. Do not ever harp in the sadness of those who leave unexpectedly. However, rejoice in knowing those who are meant will always stay. When we are able to comprehend and acknowledge the strength and worth of our tree, we will no longer allow ourselves to freely open ourselves up to the likes of everyone. Knowing the strength of our tree will teach us the value of who we are and only in that will we be able to operate in pure excellence, our greatest gifts, and the God-like individual we were created to be.

Roots Versus Branches Prayer

Dear God,

We come to You first to thank You for Your love and protection. God, we know and understand that everyone that comes into our lives is not eternal figures in our lives. Teach us how to know the difference and separate temporary from everlasting. Give us a discerning spirit and give us the strength and obedience to listen to Your voice. We know Lord, that You made us exactly in Your image and we were born into royalty before knowing who we were. Teach us to love ourselves as the Kings and Queens that we are. For so long Lord, we have ignored your voice, the warning signs You gave us, and the discerning spirit You placed inside of us. We made decisions without consulting You and now we have lost the ability to distinguish the roots in our lives versus the branches in our lives. Help us, guide us, and deliver us from those who mean us no good. Hug us tight Lord and remind us we are loved by the most high! Every time we feel lonely, less than, or inadequate, remind us of Your love for us so that we will no longer ever prefer the forged love of others versus the true love we have in You. It is not always easy but, teach us to wait for You and trust that Your will is above us and it will be all that we could and could not imagine it to be. For that sister and brother that has no direction right now, provide it for him/her Lord. Bless us to not ever lose our roots again.

In Jesus name,

Amen!

Roots Versus Branches Activity

In this activity, you will consider those closest to you. You will ponder on the family, friends, coworkers, etc., that you share a relationship of some form with. Are they a root or a branch? Refer back to the previous devotional and list the actions they display, jot down the thoughts you have had about them. Think about the warnings or positive thoughts you have had about them, write them down. Any actions, thoughts, or feelings that you have had about the person, write it down. Be honest! From here, it should be perfectly clear whether this person is a *Root* or a *Branch*.

Name:	*Name:*	*Name:*	*Name:*	*Name:*
Actions:	*Actions:*	*Actions:*	*Actions:*	*Actions:*

Jasmine D. Felder, M.Ed

Name:	*Name:*	*Name:*	*Name:*	*Name:*
Actions:	*Actions:*	*Actions:*	*Actions:*	*Actions:*

Day Ten

Conversations of the Heart

Being honest with yourself, I mean true honesty, is a necessity. Some many of us are living a fallacious lifestyle. Now while social media has its many positives, social media has caused us to believe the glitz, the glam, the likes, the comments, and the shares are what truly matters. Many of us become accustomed to proving a point that we actually do not make the point. We partake in certain activities as long as it's popular. We place ourselves in debt to appear to be in a financial bracket we are not in. We misuse individuals who want greatness for us to get ahead.

Life is not a straight or narrow road. We face so many curves, bumps, and hills that make us question who we are. Before we can become who we are destined to be, we must be honest with ourselves. We need to open up the most genuine conversations we can with ourselves and be honest about where we are. The individuals we choose for romantic relationships, are they identical to our parents? Are they identical to the parent we despise? Are we looking for love because we never received it? Do we know what love is? I can assure you that before a question is asked, we tend to know the answer. I can assure you the red flags that are thrown we see, we just ignore. Finally, I can assure you that we can see the ending of a situation if there is one before it happens.

Are we hurting ourselves purposefully? I do not believe so. I do believe our internal desire for the lives we have dreamt of and have imagined living supersedes the truth of our current moments. How long do we cry? How long do we deny ourselves? How long do we say "yes" when we mean "no"? How many times do we take the quieter approach when we should stand up for ourselves? There is no "perfect" life; however, living in the will and desire of God will give us the life worth living here on Earth. Yes, there will be many ups and downs. Tears and sorrow. However, there will be even more laughs, smiles, excitement, and joy. Do not become mesmerized by the fairy tales because they do not exist. Trust in the process. Be engulfed, wrapped up, tied up, and tangled up in God's love. Go through the twists and turns and believe in yourself. Never again hush, never again be quiet when your voice should be heard, never again ignore the questions you have, and never again turn off your light for someone else.

Final Prayer

Dear God,

All seeing and all knowing, we have encountered so much Father. We have become tired because of the physical, mental, emotional, financial, and spiritual battles we have faced. We have felt less than again society's standards without acknowledging the true power and worth we have. Remind us of who we are in You. Order our steps, so we do not continuously make the same mistakes. Encourage our visions that You have planted. Place the right people in our lives and remove the people who hold no value to us. Step in and pull us away from situations that will only drain us. Teach us to walk in Your ways to prevent unnecessary hurt and pain. Give us the desires of our hearts. Help us to forgive our old selves and deliver us from US. For those searching for a relationship with You, let them know the relationship can be what they desire it to be. As we grow into this next level with You, talk to our heart Lord. Make in us a new mind and a new heart. Deliver us from tainted practice methods. Make us new.

In Jesus Name,

Amen

Conversations of the Heart Final Activity

In this final activity, you will reflect on your growth. You will decipher which relationships in your lives have purpose versus those that do not hold value or only hold a temporary value. You will concentrate on your hopes and dreams and elect what decisions need to be made. This is your heart; what will you do with it? How will you protect it? What measures will you take to make sure it remains whole?

Letter to My Readers

Wow, book number two!!! A year ago, this was only a dream and now I am finishing book number two! This book was so very necessary to write, but if I can be honest, it was draining as well. Conversations of the Heart is a book that tackles real-life situations and conversations we all have in the midnight hour with God. Sometimes we cry out for help with no real idea on how we are going to achieve our goal.

On top of a pandemic, I lost my grandmother, the monarch of my family and life. I had to face many situations that I feel was and have continued to be detrimental to who I am as a woman. Losing my grandmother was a reality check I was not ready to face. It saddens me to this day and honestly, I am trying my best to understand life without her wisdom.

In addition to this enormous loss, I lost relationships and friendships. I questioned my worth, I questioned my career, and I questioned my direction in life. This is why this book is so important to me because I know not only myself but everyone faces loss, loses relationships, wonders about their career path, and prays for a better life daily.

I am elated that you all took this journey with me. It is my prayer that you can feel every tear I cried writing this book. I pray you can feel the stress I felt by delaying and delaying again my release dates because I wanted this book to have meaning and not just be another project. I hope that you feel my excitement about the growth we will attain in participating in these interactive prayers.

I pray God's anointing over you. To love God does not mean to be perfect. It means to strive daily to walk in his love and light. As long as we live in this world, we will fall short but never stay down. Never allow anyone to hold your past against you. Never allow anyone to make you feel as if you cannot make a mistake. The point is to grow from your mistakes, seeing that we know making the same mistake over and over is no longer a mistake; it is a choice. Identify your worth, know it, and walk in it. We are living in a time where people are breaking generational curses. In my immediate family, I am the first to graduate college and receive a graduate degree. Owning two businesses means the world to me and with raising a young queen, it is my job to give her the world but also show her how to own her own.

Stay #TeamMotivated!

I love you all and I am grateful for your support.

Sincerely,

Jasmine D. Felder

About the Author

Jasmine D. Felder is a woman of many hats. She is a child of God, a mother, a daughter, a friend, an educator, and a business owner.

Personally, Jasmine is a mother to her precious baby girl, who she loves dearly. Motherhood is the drive and motivation that pushes her to be successful. She desires to provide her daughter with a powerful image of true womanhood, success, and achievement.

Jasmine graduated in 2015 with a Bachelor of Science in Business and Information Technology from Middle Georgia State University. In 2018 Jasmine graduated with a Master of Business Administration in Communications from Walden University. Finally, Jasmine graduated in May 2021 with her Master of Arts in Secondary Education from Grand Canyon University.

Education is very important to Jasmine. As an educator of almost five years, Jasmine understands that knowledge evolves daily, and it is important that everyone maintains some form of education.

In 2020 Jasmine self-published her first book, "Finding Your Vision in the Darkness." With self-publishing her first book, she also founded and created her very own publishing company, Motivated Minds Publishing.

Jasmine enjoys reading and writing. She enjoys spending time with close family and friends, traveling, and encouraging others. Jasmine is excited for her next chapter of life and believes her season has arrived!

www.ingramcontent.com/pod-product-compliance
Lightning Source LLC
Chambersburg PA
CBHW070209100426
42743CB00013B/3117